SURFACE CHIC

AVON
PUBLISHERS OF BARD, CAMELOT, DISCUS AND FLARE BOOKS

Credits and acknowledgments:

We wish to thank the manufacturers of the many fine products pictured in SURFACE CHIC. They were all helpful, cooperative and generous with their time. A warm thanks to our friend and editor Page Cuddy whose time, talent and wit made this book possible. A special thanks to Barbara Binswanger for her patient research.

Photography by David Arky

Design and Illustration by Lynn Yost

SURFACE CHIC is a production of
JAMES CHARLTON ASSOCIATES.

SURFACE CHIC is an original publication of Avon books. This work has never before appeared in book form.

AVON BOOKS
A division of
The Hearst Corporation
1790 Broadway
New York, New York 10019

Published by arrangement with the author
Library of Congress Catalog Card Number: 84-45325
ISBN: 0-380-87478-4

First Avon Printing, November, 1984

AVON TRADEMARK REG. U.S. PAT. OFF. AND IN OTHER COUNTRIES, MARCA REGISTRADA, HECHO EN U.S.A.

Printed in the U.S.A.

DON 10 9 8 7 6 5 4 3 2

SURFACE CHIC

by

James Charlton

Anything looks better in a Tiffany box. Cut along dotted lines, fold carefully and glue.

Still wearing that passé digital watch you bought at the discount warehouse? Snap this Rolex around your wrist. You may not be able to tell time, but you'll certainly make time.

ITEMS COURTESY OF TIFFANY & CO.; ROLEX WATCHES

Cut here
Clasp
If anyone comments that this cut-and-paste jewelry doesn't look quite right, just reply that it's such a pain to get the original from the safety deposit box.
Glue
Attach with tape
Tape roll
Cut slot
Cotton
Tiffany box
Cut slot
Interlock cut slots
Impress clients and bank officers. Before you put pen to paper, wrap your pen in paper. The Mont Blanc original costs $6,500.
ITEMS COURTESY OF TIFFANY & CO.; KOH-I-NOR RAPIDOGRAPH, INC.

So you're just going to Atlanta —let them think you're flying on to Paris. Cut, fold and paste to the front of your ticket folder. On the flight home, spritz your face with Evian water and utter "how you say in English?" several times.

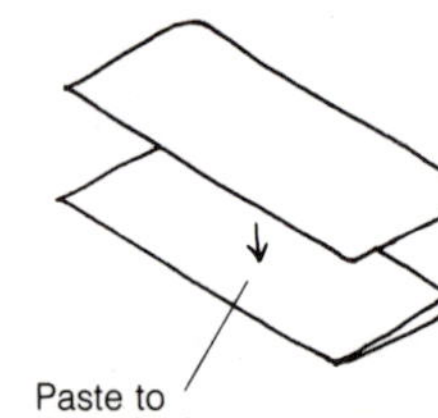

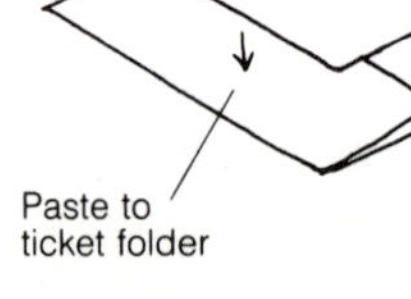

ITEMS COURTESY OF BRITISH AIRWAYS

SR 103944

swissair

SR 103944

Zurich
ZRH
Airline/Flight

The only thing more exhilarating than flying down an Alpine slope is having people *think* you did. You can have it all right here. Change the pins and tags often enough to keep them guessing.

Of course, you prefer to ski overseas, and here's the proof.

austria
american skiers' best friends

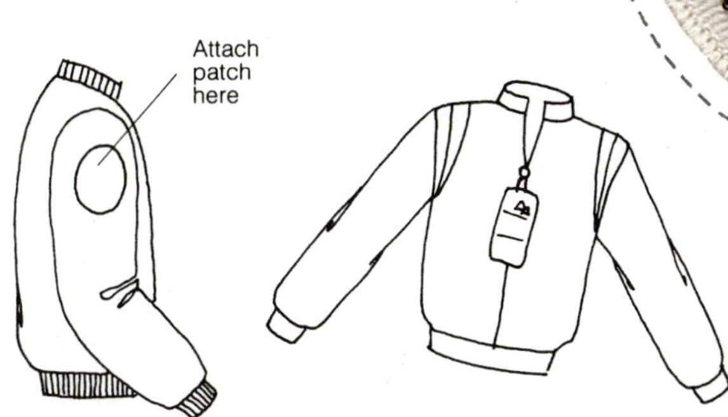

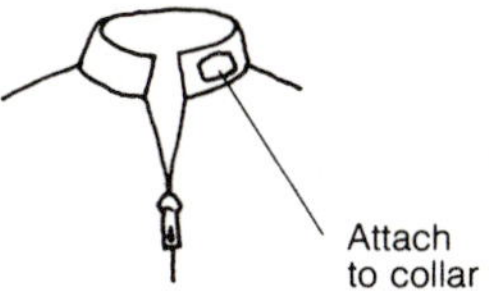

ITEMS COURTESY OF AUSTRIAN TOURIST BOARD; SWISS TOURIST BOARD; SWISSAIR

Slip this photo in the corner of your mirror. It could be you schussing.

No one will know you break out in hives at the very idea of getting on skis. Here's your lift tag and patch from, of course, Deer Valley (if they don't know it's in Utah . . .). Crunch up the lift tag to show you've taken a few spills.

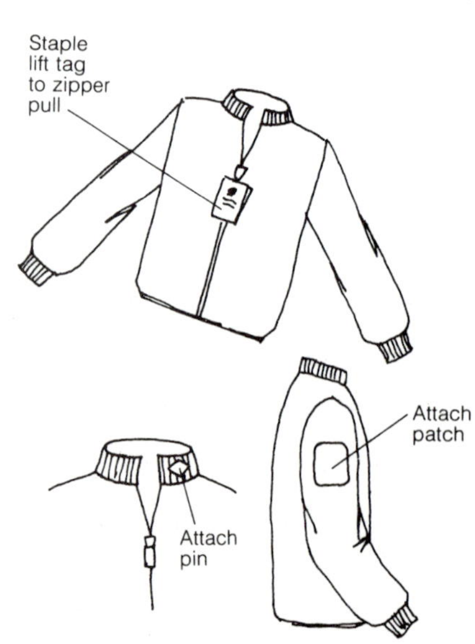
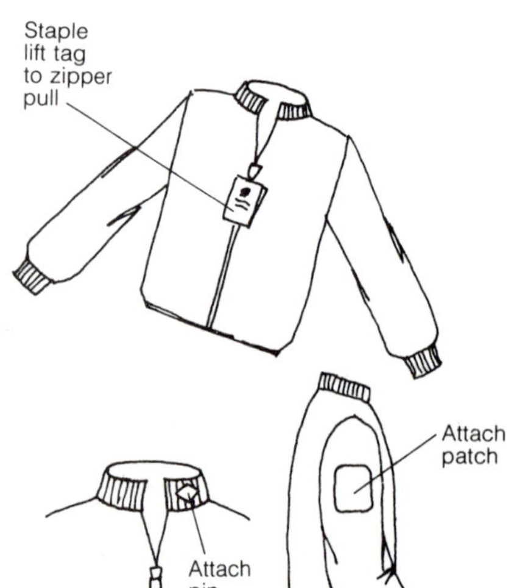

These ski buttons won't help your form, but they'll pay off back at the lodge. Fake a shoulder pain if anyone wants to touch them.

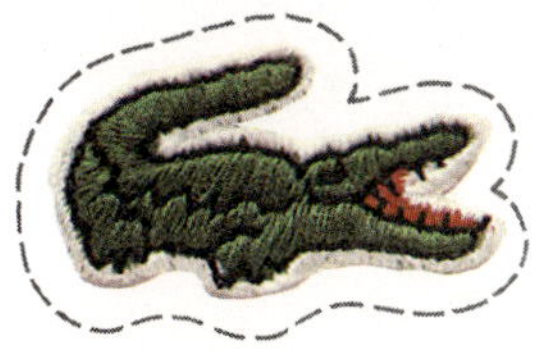

When it comes right down to it, La Coste is still the best. Just cut those other animals off your shirt and attach these classics.

BILL BLASS

Pierre Cardin

Labels and tags are important. Here are enough to punch up the drabbest of wardrobes. Be sure to put them in the proper spot so they won't be missed.

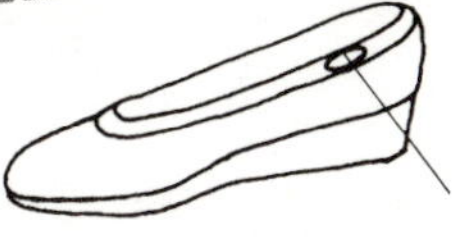

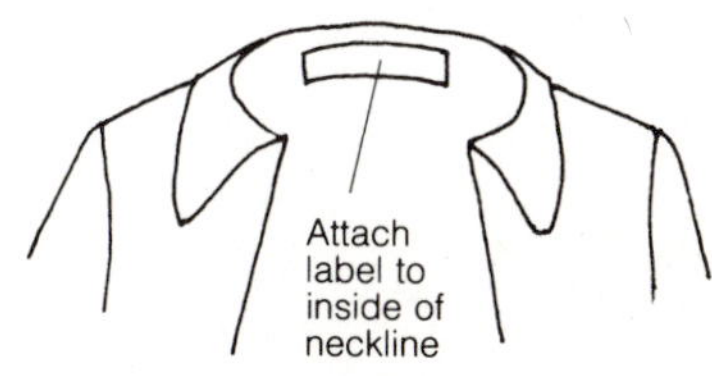

BILL BLASS

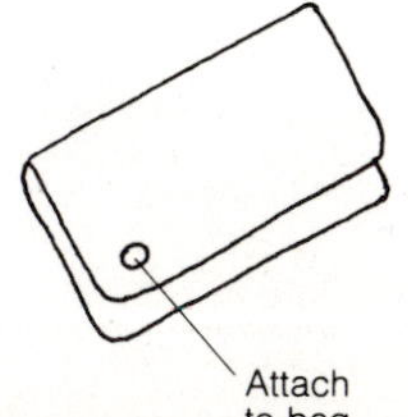

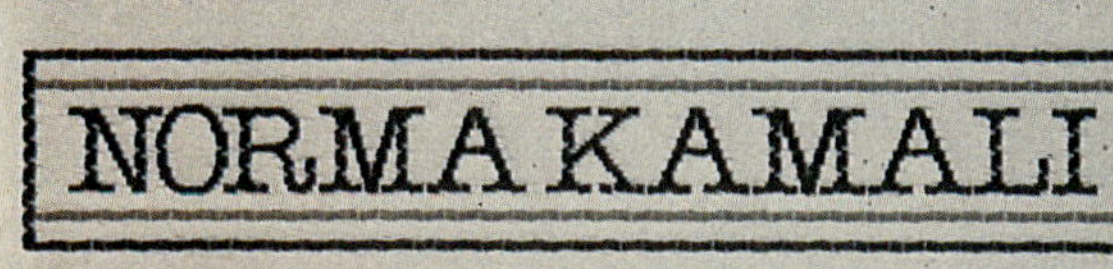

ITEMS COURTESY OF G.H. BASS & CO.; JONATHAN LOGAN, INC.; BILL BLASS; NORMA KAMALI; IZOD, LTD.; BURBERRY'S LIMITED; BRAEMAR; PIERRE CARDIN

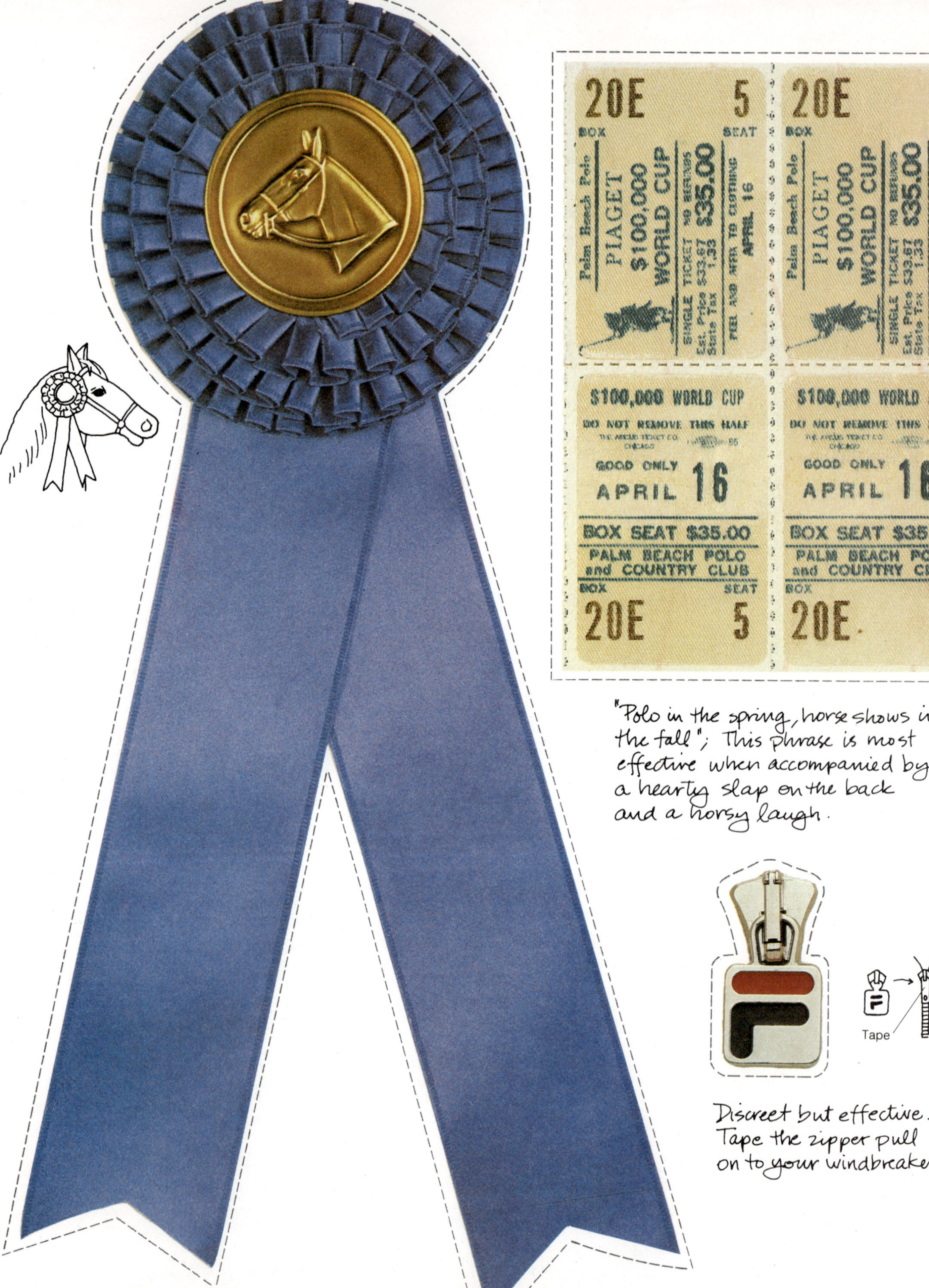

"Polo in the spring, horse shows in the fall"; This phrase is most effective when accompanied by a hearty slap on the back and a horsy laugh.

Discreet but effective. Tape the zipper pull on to your windbreaker.

ITEMS COURTESY OF FILA, PALM BEACH POLO AND COUNTRY CLUB.

The Porsche sunglasses take a bit of work, to put together, but they're worth it. And *everyone* needs an extra pair of lenses. Punch a hole in the center with a pin for viewing.

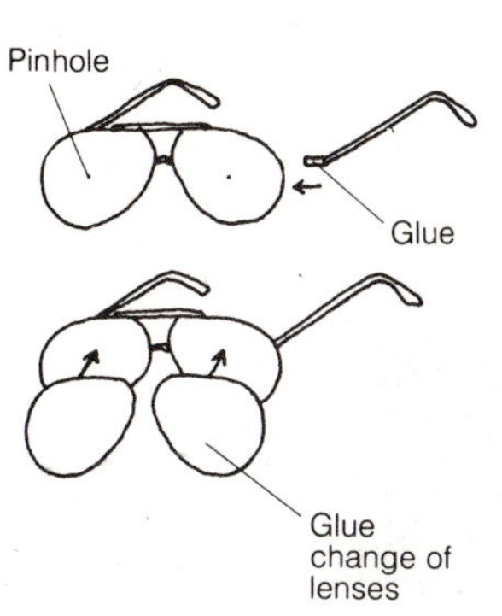

You know this sweatband is only paper, but your opponent doesn't.

ITEMS COURTESY OF CARRERA INTERNATIONAL; FILA

Notice how some guests turn over the china and crystal? This place setting for twelve will impress those hard-core voyeurs.

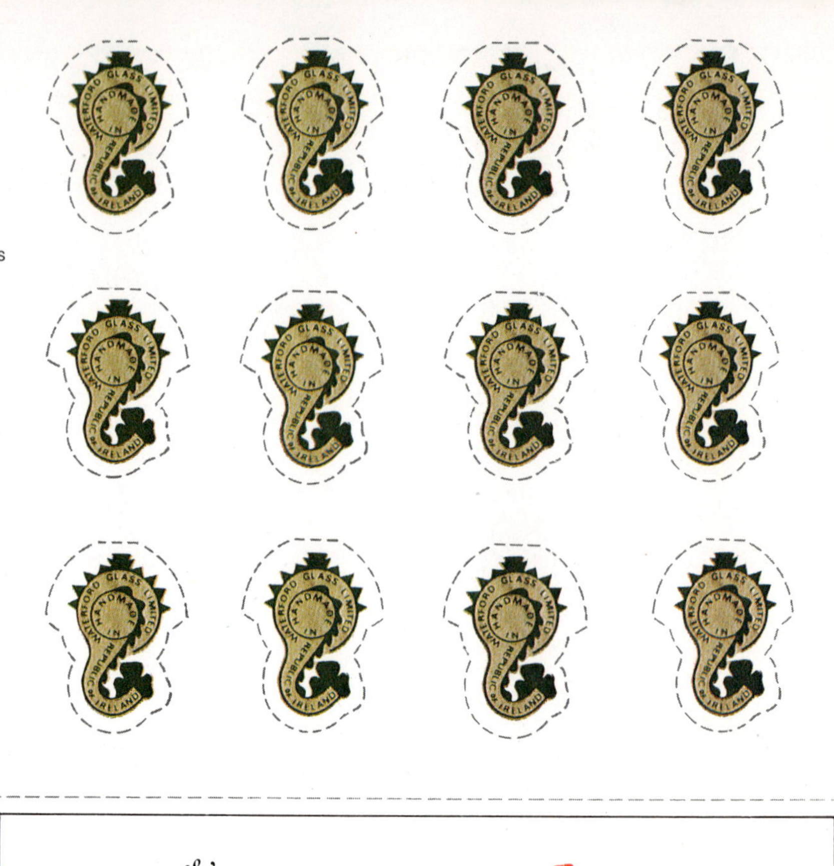

Maybe you'll never get to Studio 54, but your friends will think you're on their "A" list. Leave it on top of the junk mail pile.

This photo requires a simple silver frame, a head shot of you with a sincere but dignified smile, and possibly a short inscription from "Your good friend, Henry".

Just tape this around a cassette case, plug in a pair of earphones, and start snapping your fingers.

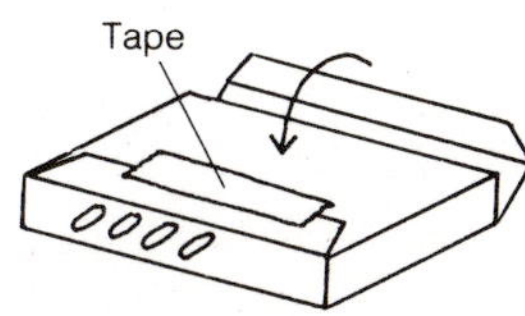

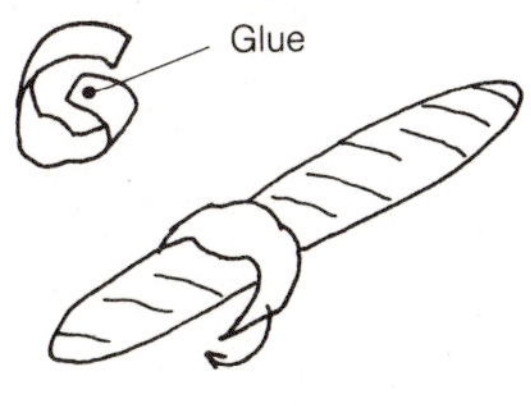

Of course you can't buy Cuban cigars in this country, but you picked these up on one of your trips abroad. Just wrap them around "three for a quarter" stogies and they'll look like they're $5 apiece.

Glue
Fold

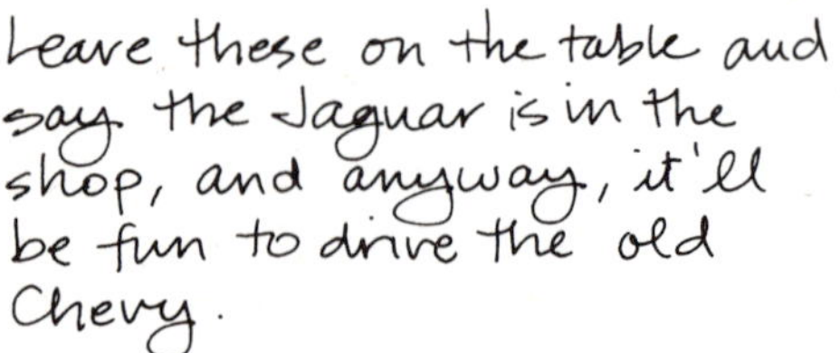

Point to the photo and talk about how your uncle plans to thrash the Aussies in the next cup race. And, if you have the time, you'll crew to help him out.

You don't have much chance to use the weekend place—don't call it a house—but it's nice to know it's there.

Expensive blooms are the ultimate chic. They cost a fortune and then die. Cut these out and mix in with the daisies.
At first glance, the place doesn't seem historically significant... and you would have expanded the two bedrooms, but you know how fussy those Landmark Commission people are...
THIS SITE
IS AN
HISTORIC
MONUMENT

Princeton ALUMNI WEEKLY

Cut out and attach to any weekly magazine and leave it in the bathroom.

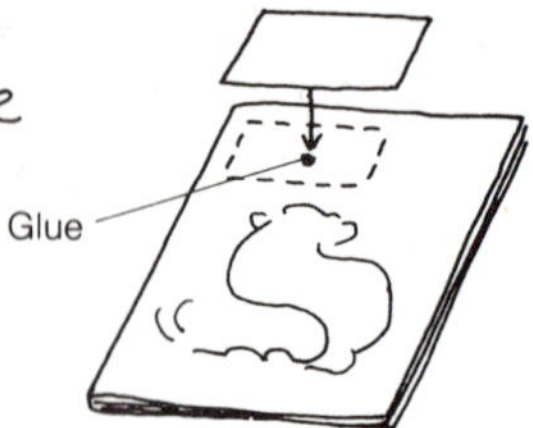

You barely got through Central High? You were an underachiever in those days. You don't like to talk about your Phi Bet pin (pronounced "Fie bait" pin) but there it is.

With these Andover buttons on your blazer, they won't even notice the jacket is polyester.

The leather bindings will fit nicely over your paperbacks, and the ticket stub makes the perfect bookmark.

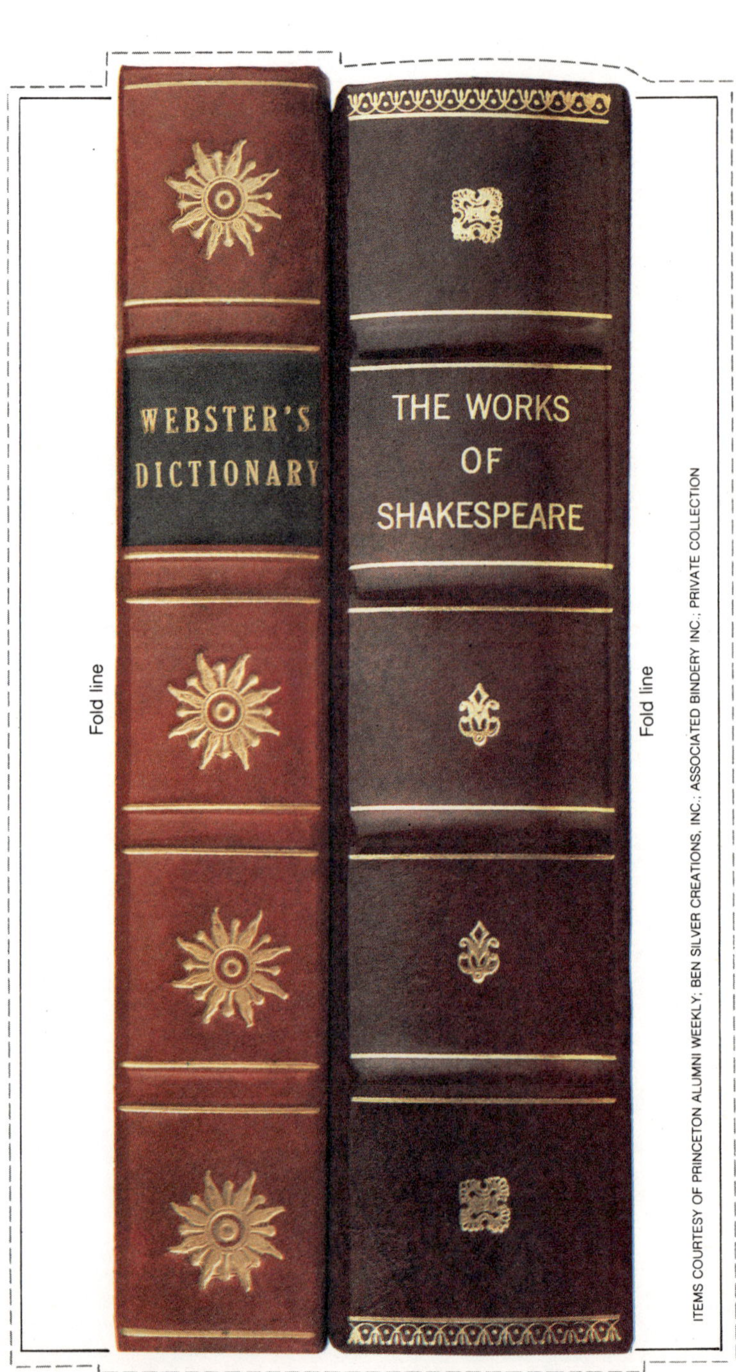

ITEMS COURTESY OF PRINCETON ALUMNI WEEKLY; BEN SILVER CREATIONS, INC.; ASSOCIATED BINDERY INC.; PRIVATE COLLECTION

ITEMS COURTESY OF PINEIDER

THE WHITE HOUSE
WASHINGTON

HOTEL DE PARIS
MONTE-CARLO

BALMORAL CASTLE

CLARIDGE'S

TELEGRAMS Claridge's London **TELEPHONE** 01-629 8860

TELEX 21872

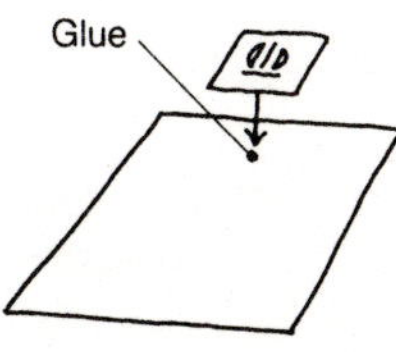

L'Ambassadeur de France près le Saint-Siège
et Madame Louis Dauge

prient ....

....

de leur faire l'honneur d'assister

.... *qu'ils donneront*

le .... *à* .... *heures* ....

Villa Bonaparte
Via Piave 23

R.S.V.P.
463 841

Is all your mail addressed to "Occupant"? Well, sit right down and write yourself a letter. Just cut out the appropriate logo, attach to white paper, and photocopy, or fill in the blanks.

Vol/Flight - Date

UT 996610

UTA French Airlines

PPT

FINAL DESTINATION

CATHAY PACIFIC
The Swire Group

BAGGAGE TAG NUMBER CX 1589245

CX 3201

FINAL DESTINATION

KUL

KUALA LUMPUR

FLIGHT NUMBER

SHANGHAI 上海

SHA

FINAL DESTINATION

CATHAY PACIFIC
The Swire Group

BAGGAGE TAG NUMBER CX 0555159

CX 3113

FINAL DESTINATION

SHA 上海

SHANGHAI 上海

FLIGHT NUMBER

ITEMS COURTESY OF UTA FRENCH AIRWAYS; CATHAY PACIFIC; HAWAIIAN AIRLINES; KONA SURF RESORT; PALM BEACH POLO AND COUNTRY CLUB; VENICE SIMPLON ORIENT EXPRESS

Fold line

Palm Beach Polo and Country Club

PBP CC

USGA RULES GOVERN PLAY
White Stakes — Out of Bounds
Yellow Stakes — Water Hazards
Red Stakes — Lateral Hazards

LOCAL RULES
No Fivesomes
Each Player Must Have A Bag & Clubs

HOLE	1	2	3	4	5	6	7	8	9	OUT
BLUE-RATING-72	364	485	157	397	419	200	436	562	378	3398
WHITE-RATING-70.5	330	460	133	378	394	173	417	538	351	3174
MEN'S PAR	4	5	3	4	4	3	4	5	4	36
HANDICAP	17	9	15	7	1	11	3	5	13	
+/− BEST BALL										
RED-RATING-72.4	297	427	109	352	375	149	375	438	309	2831
LADIES' PAR	4	5	3	4	4	3	4	5	4	36
HANDICAP	13	1	15	9	3	17	7	5	11	

Player ______________ Scorer ______________

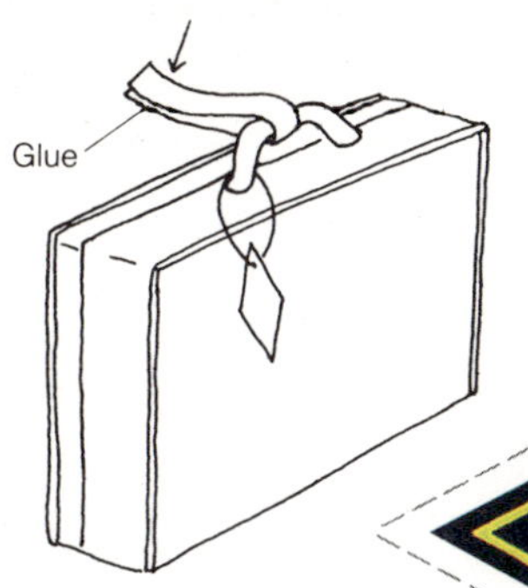

PACIFIC
JL
MPUR
TAG NO.
89245

KUALA LUMPUR

CX 1589245
(BAGGAGE IDENTIFICATION TAG)

This is not the Luggage Ticket (Baggage Check) as described in Article 4 of the Warsaw Convention or the Warsaw Convention as amended by the Hague Protocol 1955.
NOTICE: If any irregularity has occurred with respect to your checked baggage, please report it to the carrier before leaving the airport. This will assist in giving the matter prompt attention. Baggage checked subject to tariffs, including limitations of liability, therein contained.

CATHAY PACIFIC AIRWAYS LTD.

HAWAIIAN AIR
KONA, HAWAII
KOA
CHECK HERE IF BAG IS RECEIVED DAMAGED ☐

PACIFIC
HA
上海
TAG NO.
5159

SHANGHAI 上海

CX 0555159
(BAGGAGE IDENTIFICATION TAG)

This is not the Luggage Ticket (Baggage Check) as described in Article 4 of the Warsaw Convention or the Warsaw Convention as amended by the Hague Protocol 1955.
NOTICE: If any irregularity has occurred with respect to your checked baggage, please report it to the carrier before leaving the airport. This will assist in giving the matter prompt attention. Baggage checked subject to tariffs, including limitations of liability, therein contained.

CATHAY PACIFIC AIRWAYS LTD.

They think you were in Chicago. Wrap one of these around your briefcase handle before you get into the office Monday and listen to the eyebrows arching. Be careful to remove before your next flight—or you'll be in Omaha and your luggage will be in Kuala Lumpur.

DRESS CODE
Appropriate Golf Attire Required
Shirts and Shoes Must Be Worn At All Times
No Short Shorts, Tank Tops, Halter Tops
No Uniforms — Tennis, Jogging, Softball or Other
Golf Staff Will Enforce These Rules

Date

Palm Beach is a tough course, so make sure the score you fill in is not too close to scratch. Leave the card in your locker or poking out of the side pocket of your golf bag.

KONA SURF RESORT
KEAUHOU KONA HAWAII

For maximum effectiveness, use the ball marker and tee late in a close match.

The U.S. Croquet Association patch is certain to provoke attention. Just sprinkle your conversation with terms like "peels" and "roll shots".

Glue to any silver bowl and display on a top shelf, readable but untouchable.

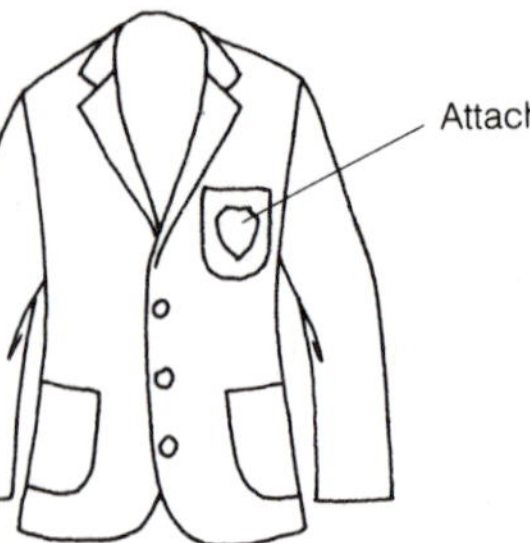

Paste on wall with wheat paste

Tape roll

This limited edition Harry Winston croquet pin can be used alone or with the patch. A tape roll will hold it in place.

Paste this Boulton system control panel to your living room wall, and no one will know the entire house isn't wired for sound.

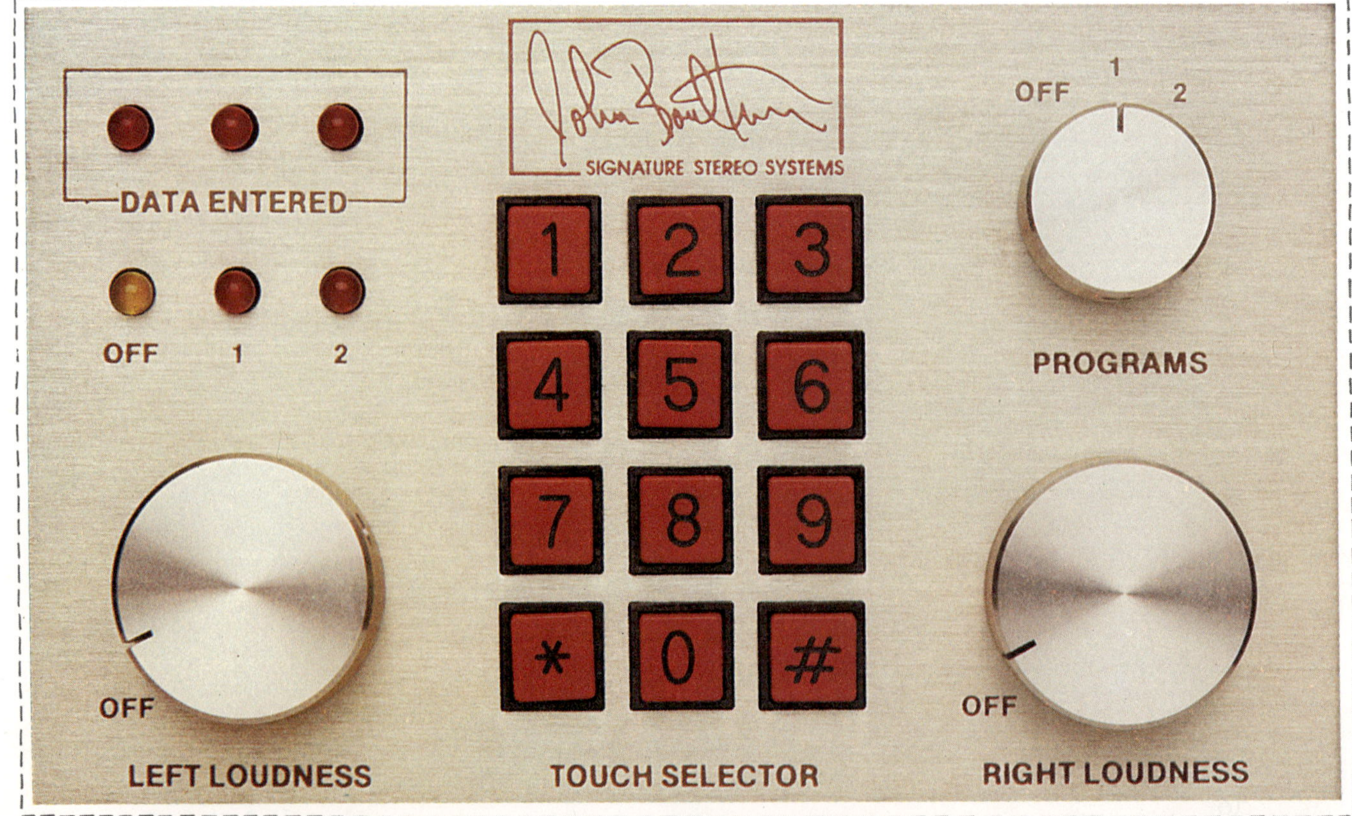

ITEMS COURTESY OF HARRY WINSTON; UNITED STATES CROQUET ASSOCIATION; BOULTON STEREO SYSTEMS

Regent Air is the most expensive way to fly to the coast, but it is the ne plus ultra, yes?

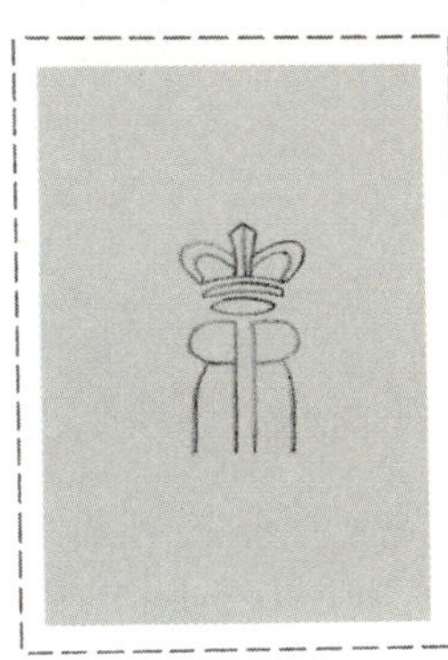

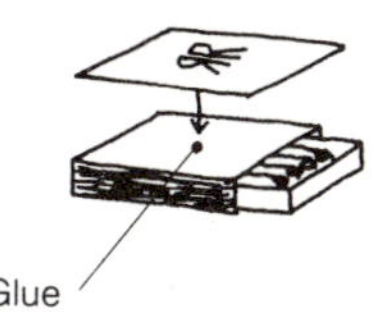

So what if you can't really see the Star Trek reruns on this—you'll look good doing it.

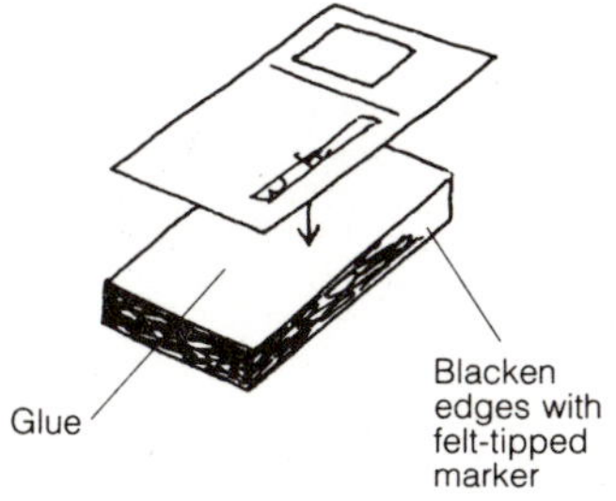

The scuba card goes in your wallet, the sticker on your luggage, and you don't even have to get your hair wet.

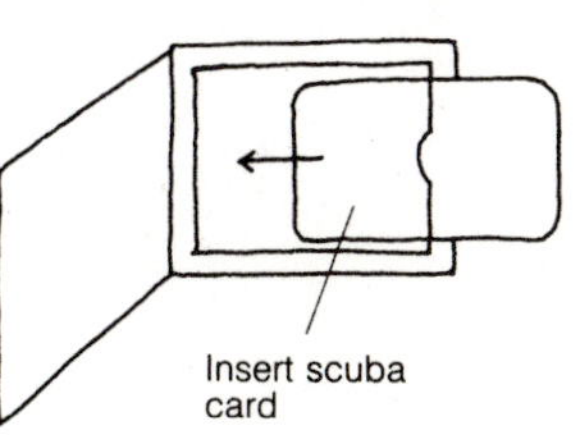

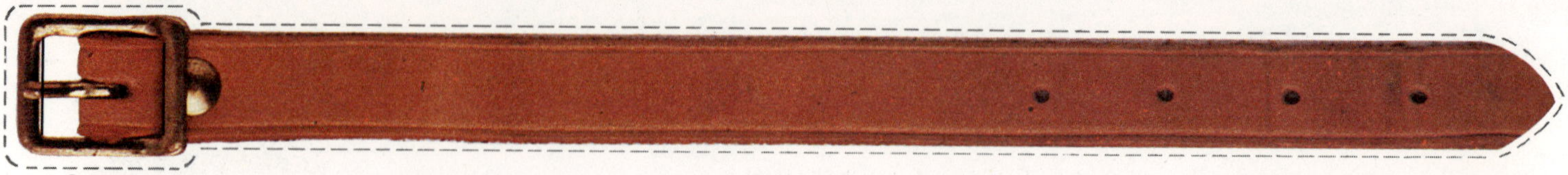

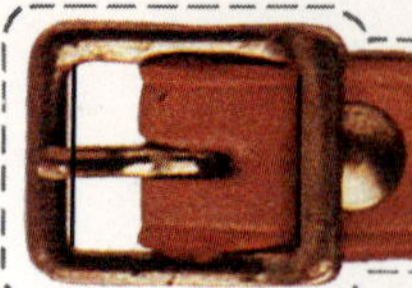

Cut slits

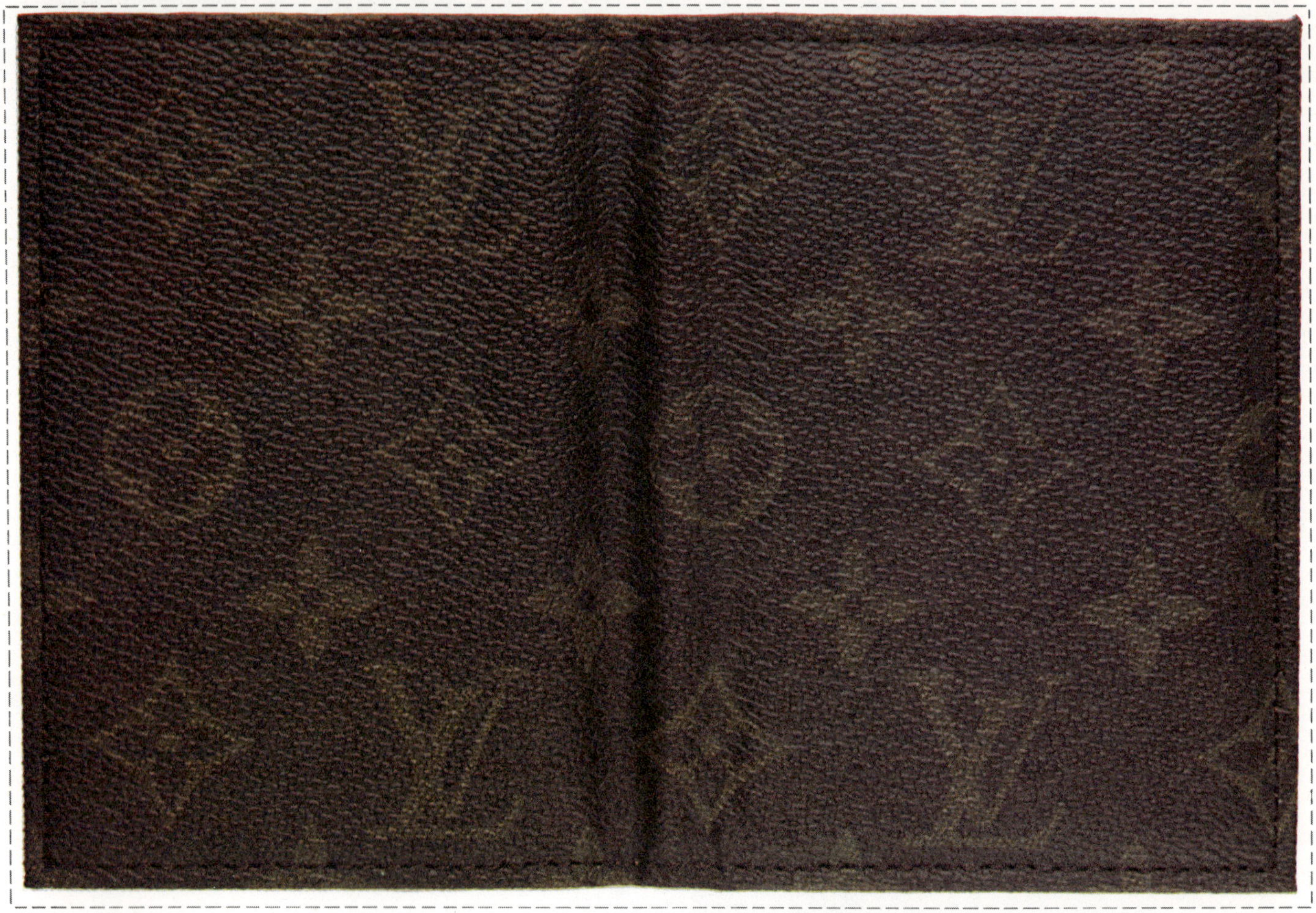

ITEMS COURTESY OF LOUIS VUITTON

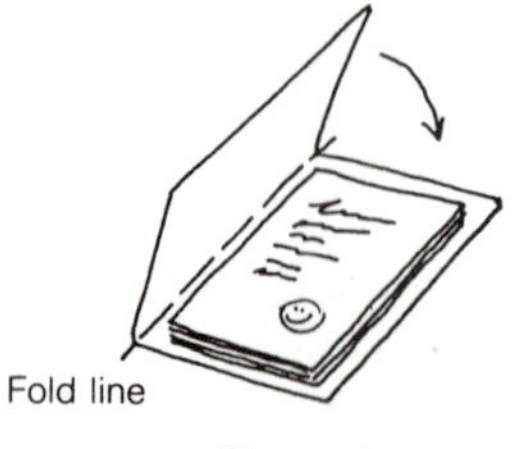

Fold line
Glue pad to cover with rubber cement

Cut out

Fold line

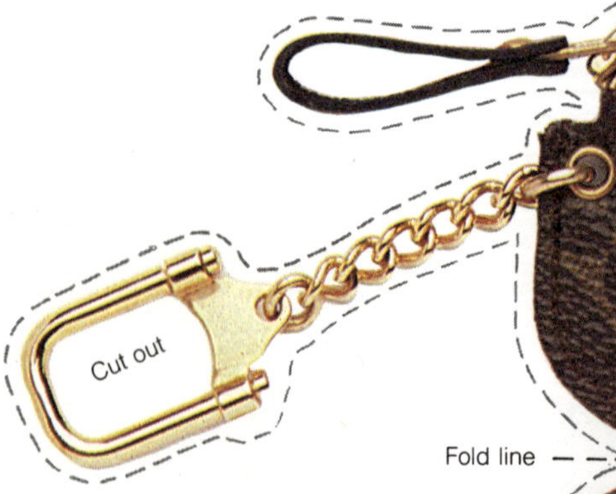

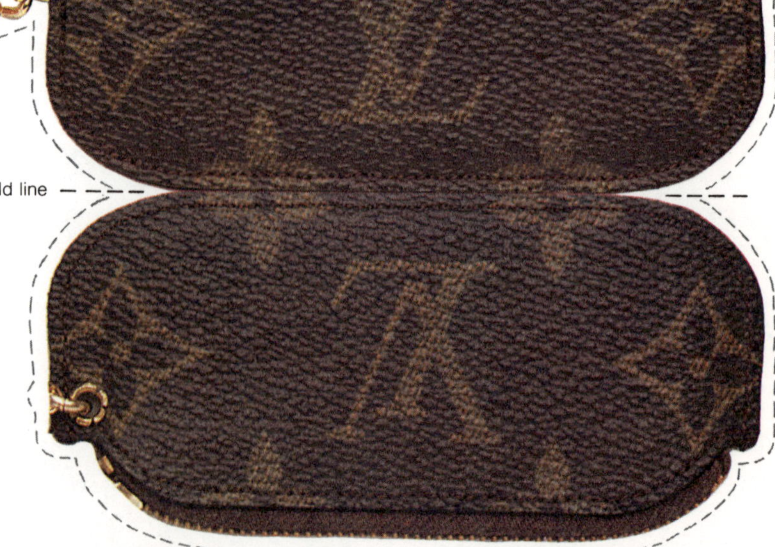

Louis Vuitton. Need we say more? The key ring is most effective with Jaguar keys. Just cut, fold and glue edges.

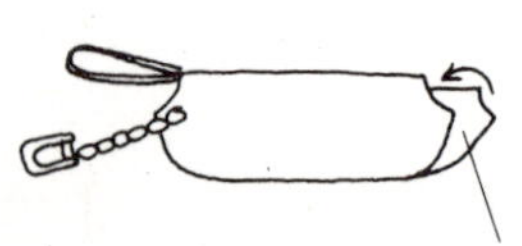

Glue

Put your name in this luggage tag, along with a two-word town (Bal Harbor or Palm Springs, for example). Never put a street address and just hope you never lose your luggage.

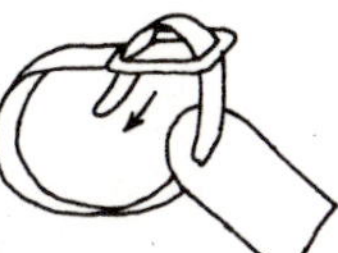

Pull through cut slots

This calculator doesn't work, but it will look good in your wallet. If necessary, complain about the light not being strong enough to power the solar cell.

Yes, you were born with the skin of a Hungarian Countess but Erno Laszlo deserves some credit.

The Erno Laszlo Institute

SKIN CLASSIFICATION

11:30

This Ghurka wallet won't hold up as well as the original, but pull it out at Lutèce and you'll get the front table. Wrap it around your old wallet and hold in place with two-sided tape or a tape roll.

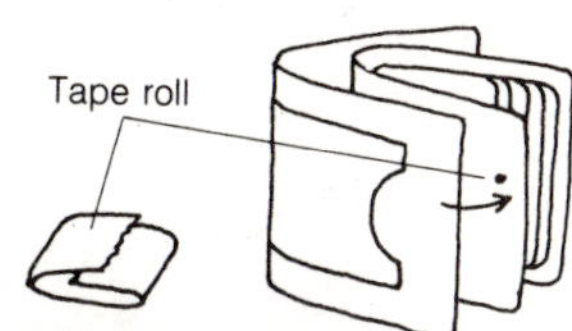

ITEMS COURTESY OF AMERICAN EXPRESS; ERNO LASZLO INSTITUTE; GHURKA COLLECTIONS

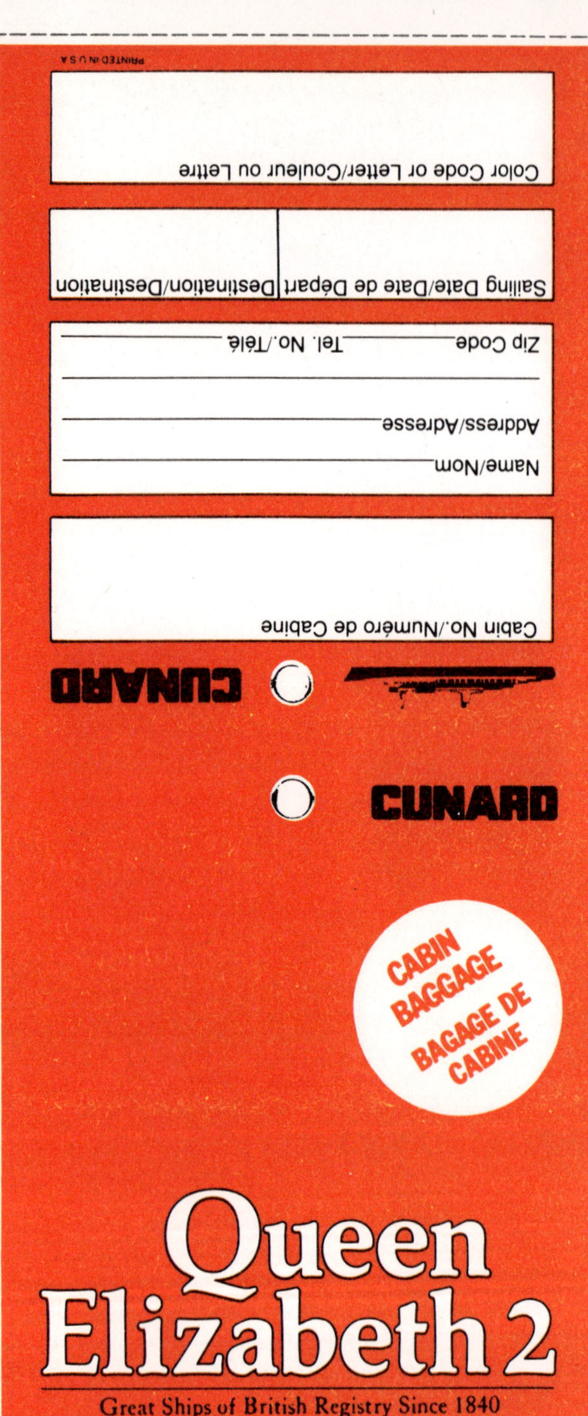

Fold line

This patch is most effective when used off the court. It looks best on a clean white, but worn, tennis shirt. Can be stitched, glued, or taped in place.

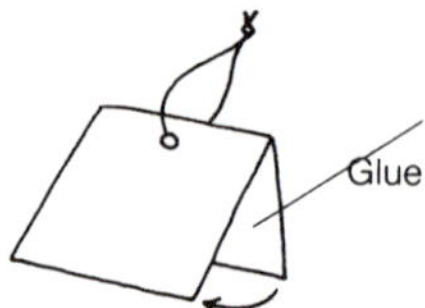

If one has the time, an ocean cruise is still the way to travel. Tie this onto a shoulder strap.

Just an old luggage tag left over from that Antarctic trip —Linblad only does exotic.

Glue

ITEMS COURTESY OF CUNARD LINES; LINDBLAD TRAVEL, INC.; HARRY HOPMAN'S INTERNATIONAL TENNIS

ITEMS COURTESY OF JOHN GARDINER'S TENNIS RANCH ON CAMELBACK; TECTEL INCORPORATED; CATHAY PACIFIC

Two weeks at John Gardiner's tennis camp and you straightened out your backhand and won these blazer buttons from John himself.

Of course you don't travel first class all the time...

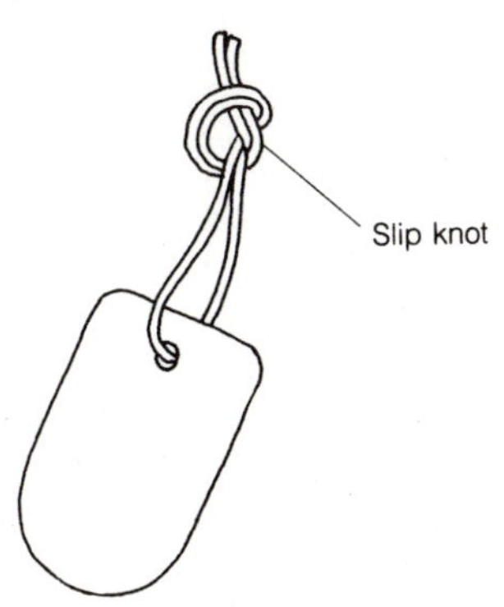

If your friends ask you why this phone never rings, tell them it's your unlisted number. Leave casually on a side table.

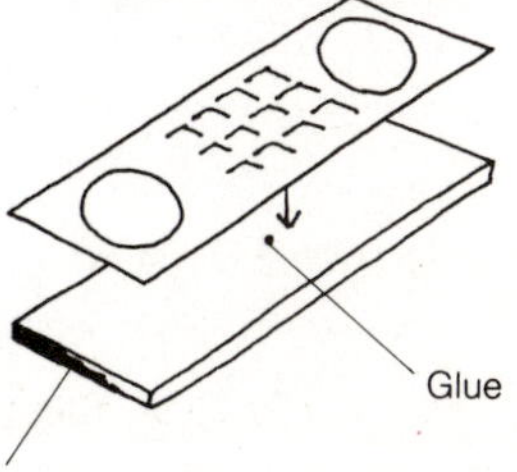

OPIUM
Parfum
YVES SAINT LAURENT

Niki de Saint Phalle
FIRST EDITION

YSL

ITEMS COURTESY OF OPIUM, YVES SAINT LAURENT, CHARLES OF THE RITZ GROUP, LTD.; NIKI DE SAINT PHALLE, JACQUELINE COCHRAN, INC.; RUFFLES, OSCAR DE LA RENTA, PARFUM STERN, INC.; LAUREN, WARNER COSMETICS, INC.

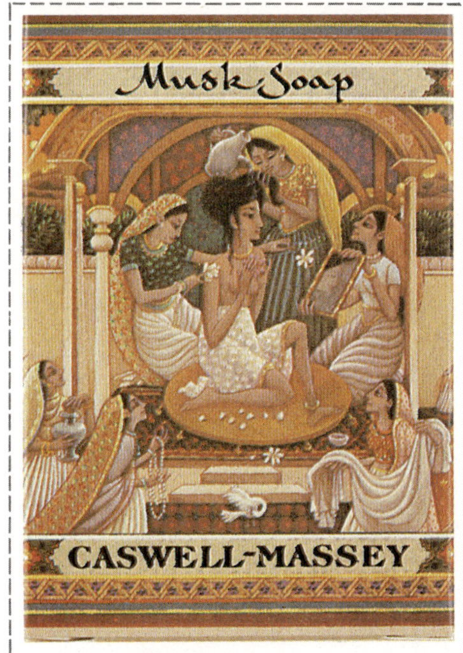

The $200 badger hair shaving brush will make any medicine shelf look better. The soaps and cologne add a lovely splash of color.

As with everything else your medicine cabinet should make a statement. These can be used singly or all in a row. Place an aspirin bottle in front to heighten the effect.

ITEMS COURTESY OF CASWELL-MASSEY

Possibly the Picasso label was prettier, but the Chagall was a much better year. Soak off label and replace with this...

Tell your guests that the baron dropped this bottle off on his last trip through town.

This New York restaurant tops its tortes with this Swiss chocolate medallion. Do the same with yours. Remove before eating.

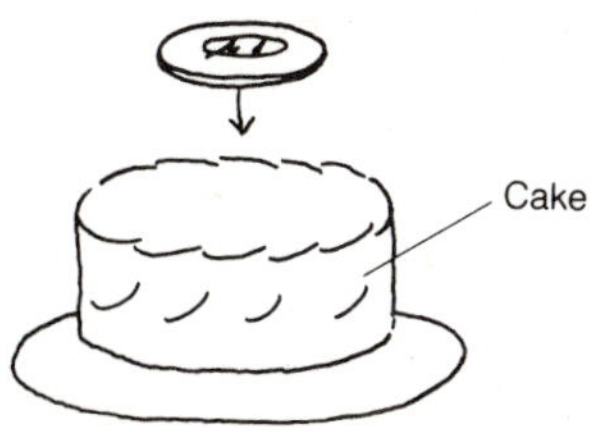

So what if the real thing isn't inside? The box is beautiful enough. And it's perfect with the Henriot champagne you're giving her.

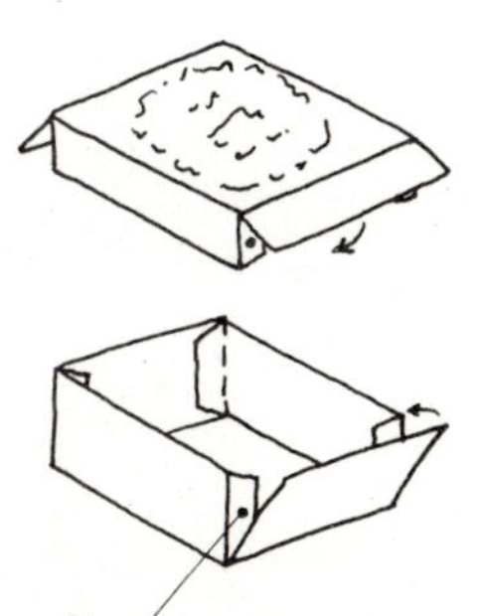

ITEMS COURTESY OF GODIVA; BUCKINGHAM CORPORATION; CAFÉ DES ARTISTES

These labels work wonders with generic bottles of various shapes. First, soak off the original label, then glue one of these on. Make sure that the label matches what's inside the bottle; it wouldn't do to put the blueberry vinegar label on a catsup bottle.

Voila! A designer cupboard!

ITEMS COURTESY OF DEAN & DELUCA IMPORTS INCORPORATED; THE SILVER PALATE

Gold goes with everything. Use the doily separately or as a complement to your condiments. Looks good on the card tray. (title page).

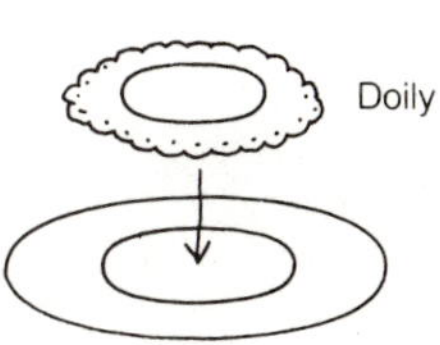

There are other places, but Claridges is the only place you stay when in London.

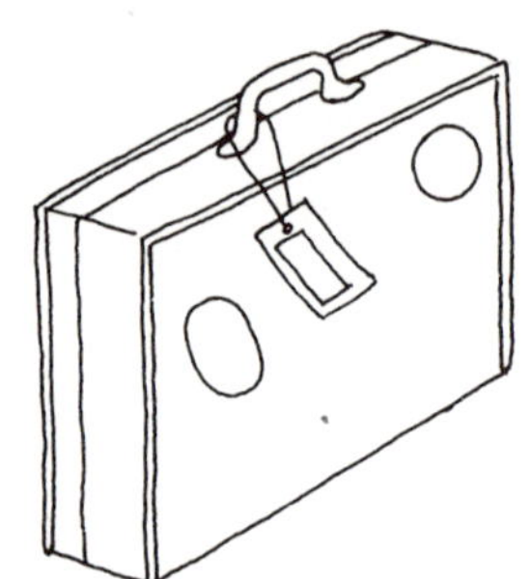

Glue

Two wonderful old hotels —your family's been going there for generations. Slip these around the handle of that Gladstone bag your grandfather owned.

Maybe you didn't stay at the Plaza suite; you used the family's pied à terre instead and just lunched in the Oak Room.

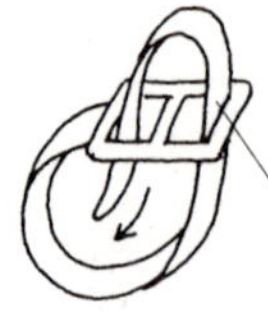

Put through cut holes

Cut out

Cut out

ITEMS COURTESY OF CLARIDGE'S; GRAND HOTEL; THE PLAZA; HOTEL PLAZA ATHÉNÉ; PRIVATE COLLECTION

Kahala Hilton HONOLULU

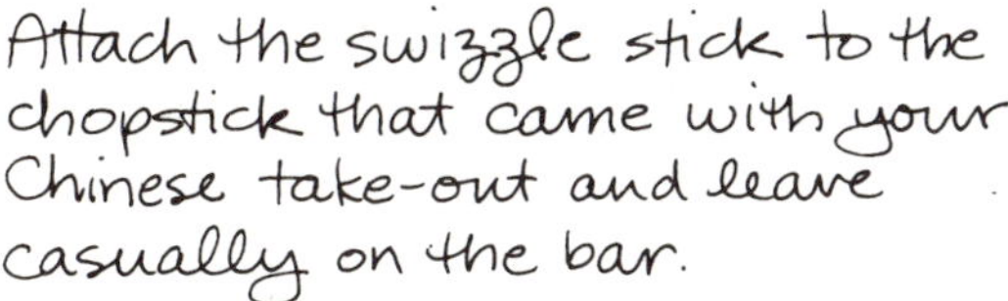

Attach the swizzle stick to the chopstick that came with your Chinese take-out and leave casually on the bar.

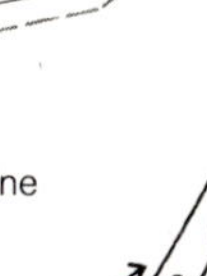

A few mementos from your many trips here and abroad. Now what year were you on that safari?

Attach the patch to a clean white apron and wear when serving your guests. If anyone dares criticize the food just give them a withering stare, curl your lip and say, "That's the way Henri taught me when I was an apprentice salad chef one summer."

ITEMS COURTESY OF SAFARI TRAVEL INTERNATIONAL; THE PEABODY; MA MAISON

RESTAURANT

Lutece

249 East 50th Street · New York City

TÉLÉPHONE 752-2225

ANDRÉ SOLTNER CHEF-PROPRIÉTAIRE
MEILLEUR OUVRIER DE FRANCE

AMERICAN ACE™ BY UNIVERSAL MATCH CORP. NEW YORK

Fold line

Fold line

Fold line

Fold line

Cut out and glue around supermarket matches. They are for boxed and regular. Place on the silver tray from page one for display.

Glue